THE WILD WORLD OF ANIMALS

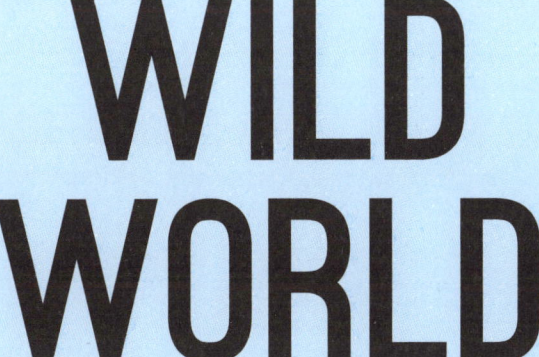

This edition published by Parragon Books Ltd in 2016 and distributed by

Parragon Inc.
440 Park Avenue South, 13th Floor
New York, NY 10016
www.parragon.com

Copyright © Parragon Books Ltd 2015-2016

© 2016 Discovery Communications, LLC. Discovery Kids, DiscoveryFacts and related logos and indicia are trademarks of Discovery Communications, LLC, used under license. All rights reserved. discoverykids.com

Written by Steve Parker
Edited by Grace Harvey
Consultant: Gerald Legg, PhD

Illustrated by Genie Espinosa
Designed by Duck Egg Blue and Alex Dimond
Production by Charlene Vaughan

All rights reserved. No part of this publication may be reproduced, stored in a retrieval system, or transmitted, in any form or by any means, electronic, mechanical, photocopying, recording, or otherwise, without the prior permission of the copyright holder.

ISBN 978-1-4748-2981-6

Printed in China

THE WILD WORLD OF ANIMALS

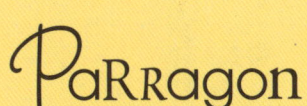

Bath • New York • Cologne • Melbourne • Delhi
Hong Kong • Shenzhen • Singapore • Amsterdam

Contents

6	What is an animal?	38	Zebra
8	Animal kingdom	40	**Polar regions**
10	What's a habitat?	42	Keeping warm
12	**Tropical rain forests**	44	Polar bear
14	On the move	46	Speedy swimmers
16	Toucan	48	Emperor penguin
18	Out of sight	50	Food in the sea
20	Orangutan	52	**Deserts**
22	Monkey or ape?	54	Finding water
24	King cobra	56	Ostrich
26	**Grasslands**	58	Desert food
28	Life on the move	60	Camel
30	African elephant	62	Super-senses
32	Run for it!	64	**Temperate woods**
34	Cheetah	66	Tree feasts
36	Grassland food	68	Moose

70	Life underground	100	**Seas and oceans**
72	Giant panda	102	Across the ocean
74	Deep sleep	104	Great white shark
76	**Rivers and lakes**	106	Between the tides
78	Super-swimmers	108	Blue whale
80	Hippopotamus	110	Battle of the giants
82	Little and large	112	**Tundra**
84	Nile crocodile	114	Big and small
86	Changing shape	116	Snowy owl
88	**Conifer trees**	118	Happy families
90	Beaver lodge	120	Caribou
92	Siberian tiger	122	Mountain tundra
94	Pack on the prowl	124	Glossary
96	Grizzly bear	126	Index
98	Fly in, fly out	128	Answers

What is an animal?

Animals come in all shapes, sizes, and colors. Some are almost too small to see. Others are as huge as a house. But they all have some things in common.

Animals make babies, or **breed**. Some animal mothers lay eggs, others give birth to live young.

Animals **move**. They might walk, run, jump, crawl, creep, climb, slither, burrow, flap, fly, swoop, or swim!

Animals need to **eat**. Some animals are plant-eaters. Others are meat-eaters. Some eat almost anything.

Baby animals **grow**. Some take just a few weeks to grow into adults, others take many years.

Animals use their **senses** to find out about the world around them. Eyes see, ears hear, noses smell, tongues taste, and skin feels.

Animal kingdom

There are millions of different animals! Scientists use their features, such as number of legs, to group them into types. This helps us understand them better.

All animals

The animal kingdom is split into two main groups: **vertebrates** and **invertebrates**.

Humans are animals, too!

Vertebrates

A vertebrate is an animal with a backbone. There are five kinds of vertebrates: **mammals**, **birds**, **reptiles**, **amphibians**, and **fish**.

Invertebrates

An invertebrate is an animal without a backbone. This group includes insects, spiders, crabs, snails, worms, and many others.

The giant spider crab has a hard shell.

Insects, like the darkling beetle, have six legs.

The giant earthworm is long, squishy, and wriggly.

Spiders, like the tarantula, have eight legs.

Mammals
- ✓ Warm-blooded
- ✓ Covered by fur or hairs
- ✓ Mothers feed their babies on milk

Birds
- ✓ Warm-blooded
- ✓ Covered by feathers, with wings, and a beak
- ✓ Lay eggs that hatch into chicks

Reptiles
- ✓ Cold-blooded
- ✓ Scaly skins
- ✓ Most lay eggs, some give birth to babies

Fish
- ✓ Cold-blooded
- ✓ Gills to breathe underwater, fins for swimming
- ✓ Lay eggs

Amphibians
- ✓ Cold-blooded
- ✓ Lay eggs in water
- ✓ Begin life with gills
- ✓ Develop lungs as they grow into adults in order to live on land

? Which types of animals do these body parts belong to?

....

What's a habitat?

A habitat is an animal or plant's home. It is the place that provides the right conditions, such as food, temperature, and amount of water, for that living being.

Tropical rain forests grow in warm, wet areas around the Equator.

Deserts may be covered with sand, pebbles, or rocks, but they are all dry. It may not rain for many years.

Temperate woodlands are found in areas where there are cold winters and warm summers. Most trees are deciduous (they lose their leaves in winter).

I think I live in a temperate woodlands habitat!

What type of habitat do you think you live in?

....

The **polar regions** are in the far north and far south of the world. In winter, the sea can be covered with thick sheets of ice and snow.

Tundra is areas of northern land that are frozen for most of the year. It is too cold for trees to grow.

Conifer forests grow in cold parts of the world. Most of the trees have cones rather than blossom and are evergreen (they have leaves all year round).

The Equator is an imaginary line running around the center of the world.

Grasslands are in warm or hot places where there is not enough rain for trees to grow.

The water in **seas and oceans** is salty. They vary from warm to cold, shallow to deep.

The water in **rivers and lakes** is not salty. Some are no more than a trickle, others are huge!

Tropical rain forests

Rain forests are hot and wet. These are ideal conditions for life. There are more kinds of animals and plants in tropical rain forests than anywhere else in the world!

Most rain forest life is high in the canopy.

The **boa constrictor** waits in the tree. It is looking for a victim to coil around, squeeze to death, and swallow whole. Then it won't feed again for weeks.

The **jaguar** prowls along the forest floor, its claws and teeth ready to kill. Its cats' eyes see well in the dark, and it listens and sniffs for prey.

The **scarlet macaw** loves the sunshine at the top of the tallest trees. This big, bright parrot's strong beak easily cracks nuts and seeds.

emergent trees

The **howler monkey** hangs out in the tangle of upper branches (the canopy). It is well named, because its huge howls and noisy roars carry far through the forest.

canopy

The **poison dart frog** sits, unafraid, in the lower branches (the understory). Its bright colors warn others: Don't try to eat me. I'm poisonous!

understory

Some animals have colors and patterns that blend into the forest.

forest floor

Can you spot a...

red-eyed green tree frog?

owl butterfly?

emerald tree boa snake?

13

On the move

Rain forests are crowded with tree trunks, branches, twigs, leaves, flowers, and fruits. Creatures have many ways of moving around.

Who's flying high?

The harpy eagle soars above the trees, flapping and gliding. It dives to grab tasty food such as a monkey, sloth, or bird.

Who's the best climber?

The spider monkey uses its curly tail as an extra limb to hold on as it climbs from one branch to another.

Who parachutes?

The flying frog has big flaps of skin (webs) between its extra-long toes. It's like having four parachutes!

Who's a speedy crawler?

The centipede has over 50 legs. It races along by wriggling its body with a wave-like motion.

Who makes huge jumps?

The bushbaby suddenly straightens its long legs and springs into mid air to catch a yummy moth or fly.

 Grab a piece of paper and follow the steps to make an origami jumping frog.

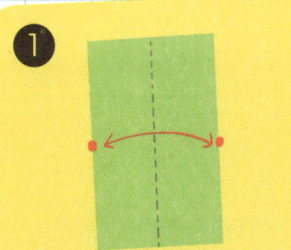

1. Fold and unfold in half lengthways.

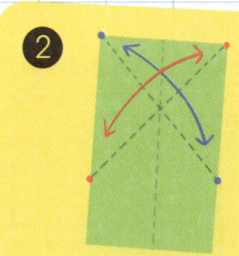

2. Fold and unfold top corners down.

3. Turn paper over. Now fold and unfold through the diagonals.

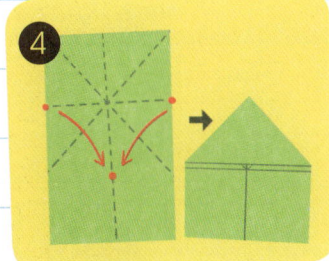

4. Turn paper over. Now pull the sides down and into the center.

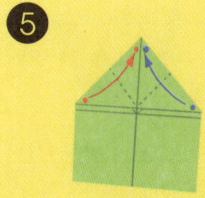

5. Fold these points upward to make the front legs.

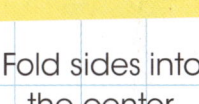 Fold sides into the center.

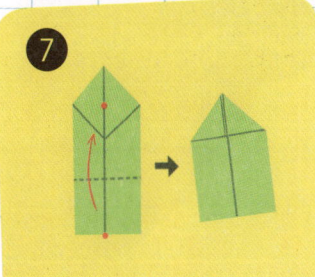

7. Fold up.

8. Fold down.

To make him jump, press down on his back!

15

Toucan

The toucan's huge beak looks heavy. But inside it's filled with hollows of air, like a sponge. This makes it lighter.

The toucan's big eyes help it choose fruits that are ripe, juicy, and ready to eat by seeing what color they are.

Toucans can be noisy! They make doggy barks and froggy croaks, and make clapping sounds by snapping their beaks together.

It's one of the biggest beaks, for the size of body, of any bird!

Inside its huge beak, the toucan has a tongue that is nearly as long, and just right for scooping out the soft middle of fruits.

ANIMAL FACT FILE

Animal group: Bird
Height: 27 inches
Habitat: Tropical forests
Where in the world: South America
Main foods: Fruits, flowers, small animals
In danger?: Yes—vulnerable

Discover the toucan's cousins. Write each bird's number in the box by its description.

Honeyguides don't have bright colors or big beaks.

Barbets have big beaks, large heads, and wide bodies.

Woodpeckers have long, sharp beaks.

Out of sight

Look quickly around the rain forest. At first, you might not see any creatures. But they are there. They are disguised as their surroundings, using a clever trick called camouflage.

Prey animals use camouflage to avoid being seen by predators!

A lump of slimy bird dropping is not what most animals want to eat. But look closer. It's actually a **bird-dropping caterpillar** in disguise.

If a **stick insect** sees a predator, it stays completely still, so it looks like the twigs around it.

Orangutan

ANIMAL FACT FILE

 Animal group: Mammal

 Height: 5 feet

 Habitat: Tropical forests

 Where in the world: Southeast Asia

 Main foods: Fruits, leaves, grubs

 In danger?: Yes—endangered

The orangutan's teeth are sharp and strong. They can pull the tough skins off fruits and crack hard seeds.

An adult male has wide cheek flaps called flanges. These make him look big and strong to females.

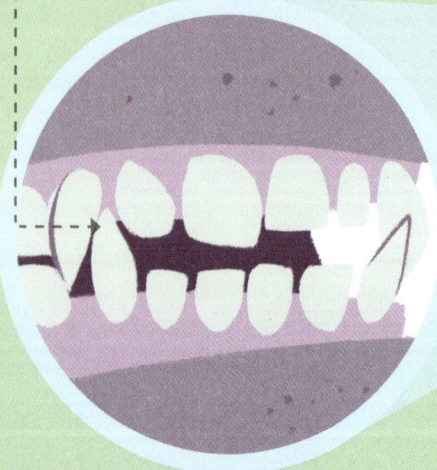

Long fur allows rain to drip off easily. In heavy downpours, this ape may even hold a big leaf over itself as an umbrella.

The clever orangutan uses thick leaves like gloves to protect its hands when picking up spiky fruit.

Can you pick a pencil up using your toes? Orangutans are able to do this easily because their big toes can touch the other toes on the same foot, just like our thumbs can touch the other fingers on the same hand.

It's harder than it looks!

The orangutan's legs bend in a similar way to the arms, and the feet grip branches just as well as the hands.

Monkey or ape?

The rain forest is noisy with the chattering, whoops, and shouts of monkeys and apes. These mammals are similar in many ways, but different in others. They both belong to the animal group called primates.

SPOTTERS' GUIDE: APES

- ✓ Apes live only in Africa and Asia
- ✓ There are about 20 different kinds of ape
- ✓ Good senses, especially big eyes for detailed vision
- ✓ No tail
- ✓ Fingers hold small objects well
- ✓ Large, heavy body, often upright

SPOTTERS' GUIDE: MONKEYS

- ✓ Monkeys live in Europe, Africa, Asia, and the Americas
- ✓ There are over 250 different kinds of monkey
- ✓ Good senses, including keen sense of smell
- ✓ Tail to help with balance
- ✓ Fingers suited to holding larger objects
- ✓ Small, light body, usually horizontal

You're on safari! Check your spotters' guides to figure out which animals are monkeys and which are apes! Write the answers below.

Clue: Native to South and Central American forests

....

Clue: The largest and heaviest living primate

....

Clue: Can easily hold small objects, like fruits

....

Clue: Uses its tail for balance when swinging through the trees

....

King cobra

ANIMAL FACT FILE

Animal group: Reptile
Length: 18.5 feet
Habitat: Tropical forests
Where in the world: South and Southeast Asia
Main foods: Snakes, lizards, rats
In danger?: Yes—vulnerable

One king cobra has enough venom to kill 20 people. Stay away!

Cobras have flaps of skin on the neck, which they spread out into a hood when they are angry.

The king cobra makes a lightning-fast bite, called a strike. Then it waits nearby for the venom to work before swallowing the victim whole.

The cobra uses two long, sharp teeth at the front of its upper jaw to bite and inject its venom. These are called its fangs. The venom can kill most creatures.

Grasslands

Did you know that grasslands can be found on every continent, except Antarctica? They grow where there is not enough rain for trees, but too much rain for a desert.

In the dry season, there's no rain for months. So the grasses gradually turn brown!

Black-tailed jack rabbit

American bison

Prairie dogs

In **North America**, areas covered with grasses are known as **prairies**.

Giant anteater

In the wet season, it rains hard, with thunder, lightning, and storms. So fresh green grass can grow!

Rhea

In **South America**, grasses can be twice as tall as you are! The name for grassland here is **pampas**.

Life on the move

Animals that eat mostly grass are called grazers. They are always on the move to find fresh green grass to eat.

A **leopard** waits for a young, old, or sick animal to get left behind.

Home den

Wildebeest stamp, snort, and grunt as they sniff the air for fresh grass.

The predators who hunt the grazers must stay on the move, too!

Waterhole

African elephant

ANIMAL FACT FILE

- **Animal group:** Mammal
- **Height:** 13 feet
- **Habitat:** Grasslands, woodlands
- **Where in the world:** Africa
- **Main foods:** Grasses, leaves, fruits, bark
- **In danger?:** Yes—vulnerable

The elephant's tail swishes away flies and other pests.

Join the dots to see who is following its mother.

An elephant can walk for days! Its long legs can take big steps.

Run for it!

Grasslands have very few trees, rocks, valleys, or other places to hide. When in danger, the best way to escape is to run fast!

A kangaroo can leap a length of 16 feet in a single hop. Ask someone to measure that along the ground. Then see how far you and your friends can long-jump!

The **white rhino** of Africa can charge for a short distance at 30 miles per hour.

Name	Distance

Cheetah

It's too fast for me to photograph!

ANIMAL FACT FILE

 Animal group: Mammal

 Length: 7 feet, including tail

 Habitat: Grasslands, scattered woodland, scrub

 Where in the world: Africa and Southwest Asia

 Main foods: Animals, from mice to antelopes

 In danger?: Yes—vulnerable

The cheetah can run at speeds of around 70 miles per hour, accelerating fast to chase down its prey.

Its tail helps a cheetah balance while it's running.

The cheetah's claws are partly out at all times to grip the ground, so it is always ready to run!

The two black lines on a cheetah's face are called "tear marks." Each line runs from the inside corner of the eye to the corner of the mouth. Finish the other side of the cheetah's face.

Don't worry! The cheetah can only keep its top speed for less than a minute.

The cheetah's body is perfectly shaped for speed. It has a super-flexible back that helps it take long, fast strides.

Grassland food

The main food in the grassland is ... grass! So it's not surprising that most food chains here start with grass stems, leaves, seeds, or roots.

AFRICA

The lion is the top meat-eater in this food chain. It hunts a plant-eater: the grant's gazelle. The gazelle eats grass leaves.

Lion

Grant's gazelle

SOUTH AMERICA

The jaguar is the top meat-eater here. It eats other meat-eaters, like the giant anteater, who eats termites. Termites are plant-eaters—they eat grass roots.

Jaguar

Giant anteater

ASIA

There are three meat-eaters in this food chain: the steppe eagle, steppe polecat, and racerunner lizard. The darkling beetle is a plant-eater that eats grass seeds.

Steppe eagle

Steppe polecat

Which foods do these animals eat? Draw lines to the correct answers.

"A food chain shows what each living thing eats!"

"Or who is eating whom!"

Grass leaves

Termites

Grass roots

Racerunner lizard

Darkling beetle

Grass seeds

Zebra

ANIMAL FACT FILE

Animal group: Mammal

Height: 7 feet

Habitat: Grasslands, scrub, and shrub

Where in the world: East and southern Africa

Main foods: Grasses, flowers, leaves

In danger?: Not yet

The zebra has very good senses. Its large eyes see far, its big ears hear faint sounds, and its long nose picks up many smells.

Its wide, strong teeth munch grasses for up to 16 hours each day.

No one really knows why zebras have stripes! Some possible reasons are:
- Maybe for camouflage, to help it hide among tall grasses and bushes.
- Perhaps to recognize each other, since every zebra has a slightly different pattern.
- Possibly to stay cool.
- Maybe to make it difficult for a predator to pick out one zebra from a group.

Baby zebras, like baby horses, are called foals.

Foals can stand up, walk, and run only one hour after being born!

Can you add the foal's stripes?

Polar regions

The polar regions are the coldest places on Earth. They are covered with ice and snow for much of the year. Despite this, wild animals manage to survive there!

Join the dots to see which white animal is riding on the iceberg.

The **hooded seal** is a speedy swimmer. It chases smaller creatures for food.

The **Northern fulmar** plunges into the water to catch shrimps, fish, and squid.

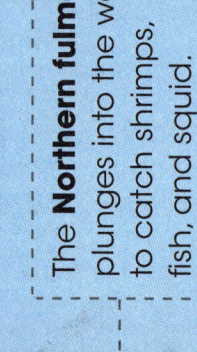

The **right whale** comes to the surface to breathe, before diving again to feed.

Arctic

North Pole (Arctic)
The Arctic is an ocean. Huge floating sheets of ice and lumps of ice, called icebergs, float across it.

South Pole (Antarctic)
The Antarctic is a huge area of land, covered with ice.

Antarctic

Wow! It's almost as big as a REAL elephant!

The **Southern elephant seal** dives deep to catch fish and squid.

The **South polar skua** flies over the ice, looking for dead fish and other scraps of food.

Chinstrap penguins gather together on an iceberg to rest.

Keeping warm

When it's cold outside, we wrap up warm! But how do polar animals keep the heat in and the cold out?

Brr! In polar regions, it's cold all year round!

GYRFALCON

The gyrfalcon is a big Arctic bird of prey. Its tough outer feathers keep out the worst weather. Beneath the outer feathers are soft, fluffy feathers, called down, to keep in its body warmth.

Feathers overlap to keep out wind

BELUGA WHALE

The beluga is a 16-foot-long Arctic whale. Under its white skin is a thick layer of fat, called blubber. The blubber works like an all-over sleeping bag, keeping the beluga warm.

ARCTIC FOX

The Arctic fox's thick fur keeps out wind, rain, sleet, and snow. It wraps its tail around itself like a cozy scarf. Even if it sleeps in the open, covered with snow, it stays warm.

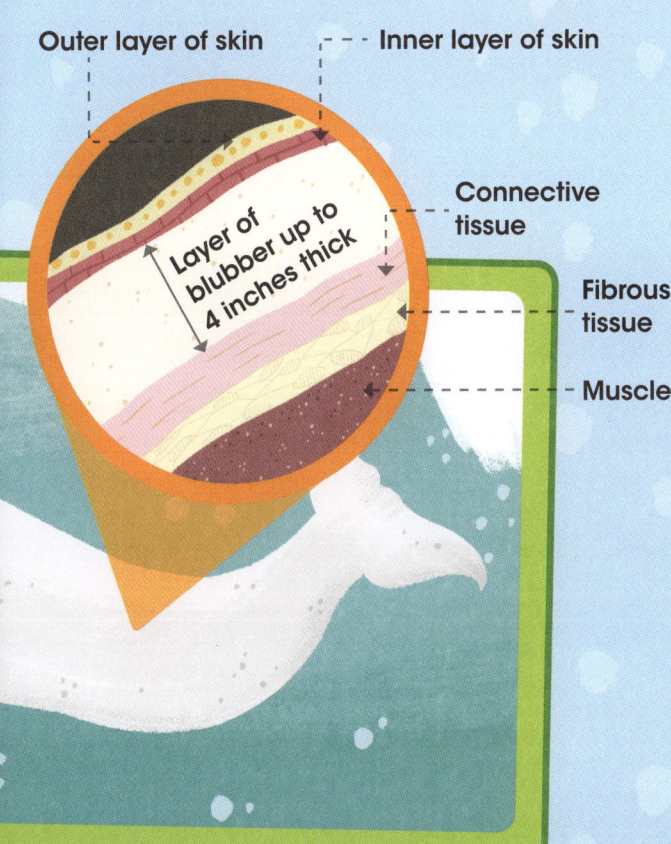

Outer layer of skin • Inner layer of skin • Layer of blubber up to 4 inches thick • Connective tissue • Fibrous tissue • Muscle

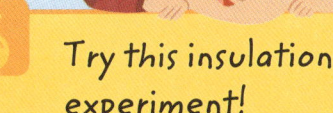

Try this insulation experiment!

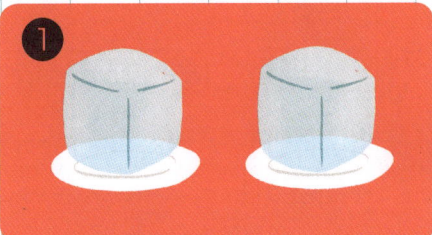

1. Take two ice cubes the same size and put each one on a plate.

2. Wrap one ice cube in material, such as a towel. Or put it in an old woolly sock or glove.

3. Put both plates in a warm place. You should discover that the ice cube that is not wrapped melts first. Why?

Polar bear

ANIMAL FACT FILE

 Animal group: Mammal

 Height: 10 feet, standing on back legs

 Habitat: Ocean, icebergs, coasts

 Where in the world: All around the Arctic

 Main foods: Seals, crabs, seabirds, fish, whales

 In danger?: Yes—vulnerable

I'd better watch out! Polar bears are the world's largest meat-eaters on land!

A polar bear's paws have hairy soles, to grip slippery ice.

Its big, sharp claws work like hooks to catch seals and other prey.

The outer layer of guard hair is long and strong. The inner layer of underfur is soft and warm.

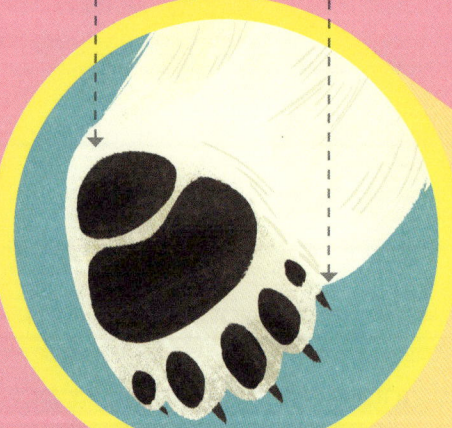

44

A polar bear can sniff the scent of a dead seal or whale from 1.2 miles away.

White fur is the perfect camouflage. It matches the ice and snow around.

Baby polar bears, called cubs, follow their mother for more than two years, copying her actions. They learn how to swim, hunt, and avoid dangers.

Most mother bears have two cubs. Draw the second one.

Speedy swimmers

Seals, fur seals, and walruses all have strong flippers for fast swimming. They belong to the animal group called pinnipeds.

The **harp seal** lives in the Arctic Ocean.

The **walrus** lives in the Arctic Ocean.

Front and rear flippers can waddle on land

True or false? Check the boxes.   TRUE FALSE

The walrus lives in the Antarctic. ☐ ☐

The fur seal has very little fur. ☐ ☐

The harp seal has sharp teeth. ☐ ☐

The walrus's long teeth are called fangs. ☐ ☐

The **Northern fur seal** lives in the north Pacific Ocean.

Fur seals make loud barks like a dog!

Emperor penguin

"The emperor weighs up to 110 pounds—probably more than you!"

Its body is smooth and streamlined for fast swimming.

The emperor penguin has a thick, fatty layer, called blubber, under its skin to keep it warm.

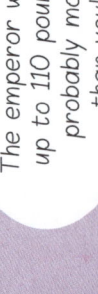

ANIMAL FACT FILE

Animal group: Bird
Height: 4 feet
Habitat: Icy places such as icebergs and frozen shores
Where in the world: Antarctica
Main foods: Fish, shellfish, squid
In danger?: Not quite—near threatened

The penguin's feathers are strong and waterproof.

Its wings are small and useless for flying. But they are fantastic swimming flippers.

The penguin spends much time preening—cleaning its feathers with its beak and feet.

Its wide feet grip ice well and stop the penguin from sinking in the snow.

Emperor penguins lay their eggs in the middle of winter. Each male balances an egg on his feet, covering it with a flap of belly skin so it does not freeze. The males gather together to keep warm. Help this dad get to the others at their nesting site.

Start

Finish

Food in the sea

In polar regions, few plants grow on land, so most food chains start in the sea!

There are 1,000 plankton in one drop of sea water!

❶ Plankton
Size: 0.04 inch
Plankton are tiny plants and animals that float in the sea. Plant plankton are smaller than this period.

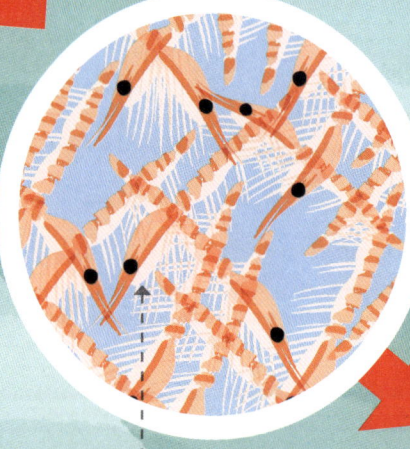

❸ Silverfish
Size: 6 inches long
Krill are hunted by Antarctic silverfish, which are fast-swimming predators of smaller creatures.

❷ Krill
Size: 1.6 inches long
Plant plankton are eaten by krill. They look like shrimps. They are small, but there are millions of them.

④ King penguin
Size: 40 inches tall
Silverfish are victims of the king penguin, which is the second largest of all the penguins.

⑤ Leopard seal
Size: 120 inches long
Penguins are common prey of the leopard seal—a slim, strong, fast, and fierce hunter.

⑥ Killer whale
Size: 350 inches long
Even the leopard seal is not safe from one of the ocean's most fearsome predators, the killer whale.

Krill swim in crowded groups called shoals. How many krill are jumbled up here?

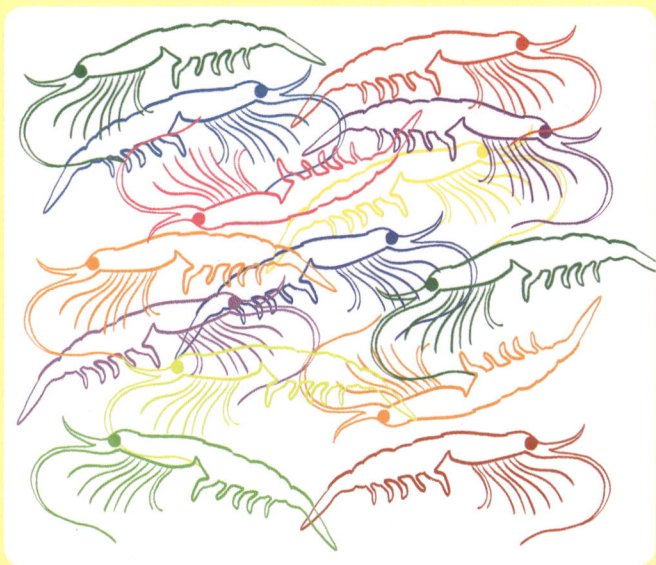

51

Deserts

Do you think all deserts are hot? Some are, but others are extremely cold! Some deserts are covered with sand, others are full of rocks. But all deserts are very, very dry.

Daytime
Most animals hide in their burrows to keep out of the sun. Some creatures wander around and look for food, although they try to stay in the shade.

The **secretary bird** walks long distances every day as it looks for its favorite foods: snakes, lizards, mice, rats, and baby birds.

The **sandfish** is not a fish, but a kind of lizard. It wriggles through the loose sand hunting insects.

Yikes! The Sahara is the largest hot desert.

🔍 The Saharan silver ant comes out of its nest during the hottest part of the day to avoid predators. Can you find five ants before they return to their nests?

Nighttime
Animals come out of their resting places to feed. It is much cooler, and the sand and rocks do not burn their feet.

The **eagle owl** looks and listens, before swooping silently onto small animals such as lizards, snakes, scorpions, mice, and jerboas.

The **jerboa** has huge ears, a long tail, and very long back legs for hopping around.

The **fat-tail scorpion** searches for prey such as insects and worms. It has powerful pincers and a deadly sting at the end of its tail.

The **darkling beetle** wanders through the sand and rocks to find seeds and plants to eat.

Finding water

In deserts, it hardly ever rains. The ground is dry for months, or even years, at a time. Only very tough plants can grow. So how do the animals survive?

I wouldn't need my umbrella in a desert!

ARABIAN ORYX

In African deserts, the Arabian oryx gets all its water from the plants it eats. It also saves water in its body by hardly ever peeing.

SPADEFOOT TOAD

In the deserts of southwest North America, the spadefoot toad digs down into loose, damp soil and waits until the rain returns.

BUDGERIGARS

In Australian deserts, small parrots called budgerigars fly long distances to waterholes. They form large flocks and stand around the water's edge to drink.

GERBIL

In Asian deserts, the gerbil stays in its burrow by day. It even blocks up the entrance with a stone or soil to keep in the moisture from its breath.

VISCACHAS

In South American deserts, viscachas live in underground burrows and tunnels. They dig deep to where the soil is damp, and lick water from the tunnel walls.

Try this water loss experiment!

❶ On a hot, sunny morning, cut out animal shapes from blotting paper and soak both of them in water.

❷ Put one animal where it will be in the sun all day. Put the other in a cool, shady place.

❸ After a few minutes, look at the animals. The one in the sun should have lost more water. This is why desert animals like to stay in the shade.

Ostrich

It uses its big, strong beak to peck and eat almost any food, from soft plants and worms to hard seeds and beetles.

The ostrich is the world's largest bird!

The ostrich lays the largest eggs, each as big as 25 hens' eggs!

The ostrich has the largest eye size of any land animal.

The ostrich is taller than a person. It can see a long way across the desert to look for food, and also to spot danger.

The ostrich's wings are too small for it to fly. But they can be waved like fans to keep the ostrich cool in the midday heat.

ANIMAL FACT FILE

Animal group: Bird
Height: 8 feet
Habitat: Deserts, grasslands
Where in the world: Africa
Main foods: Almost anything, from buds to beetles
In danger?: Not yet

The huge feet, with large toes, grip hard ground well.

Long legs allow the ostrich to run extremely fast. It can reach speeds of more than 45 miles per hour—almost twice as fast as a champion human sprinter.

Fill in the missing heights of some other big birds that cannot fly.

6 ft
5 ft
4 ft
3 ft
2 ft
1 ft
0 ft

Name:	Rhea	Cassowary	Emu
Location:	South America	Australia	Australia
Height:	……feet	……feet	……feet

Desert food

Desert food chains often include lizards and snakes. These reptiles, with their tough scales, need little water, and survive well even in the driest places.

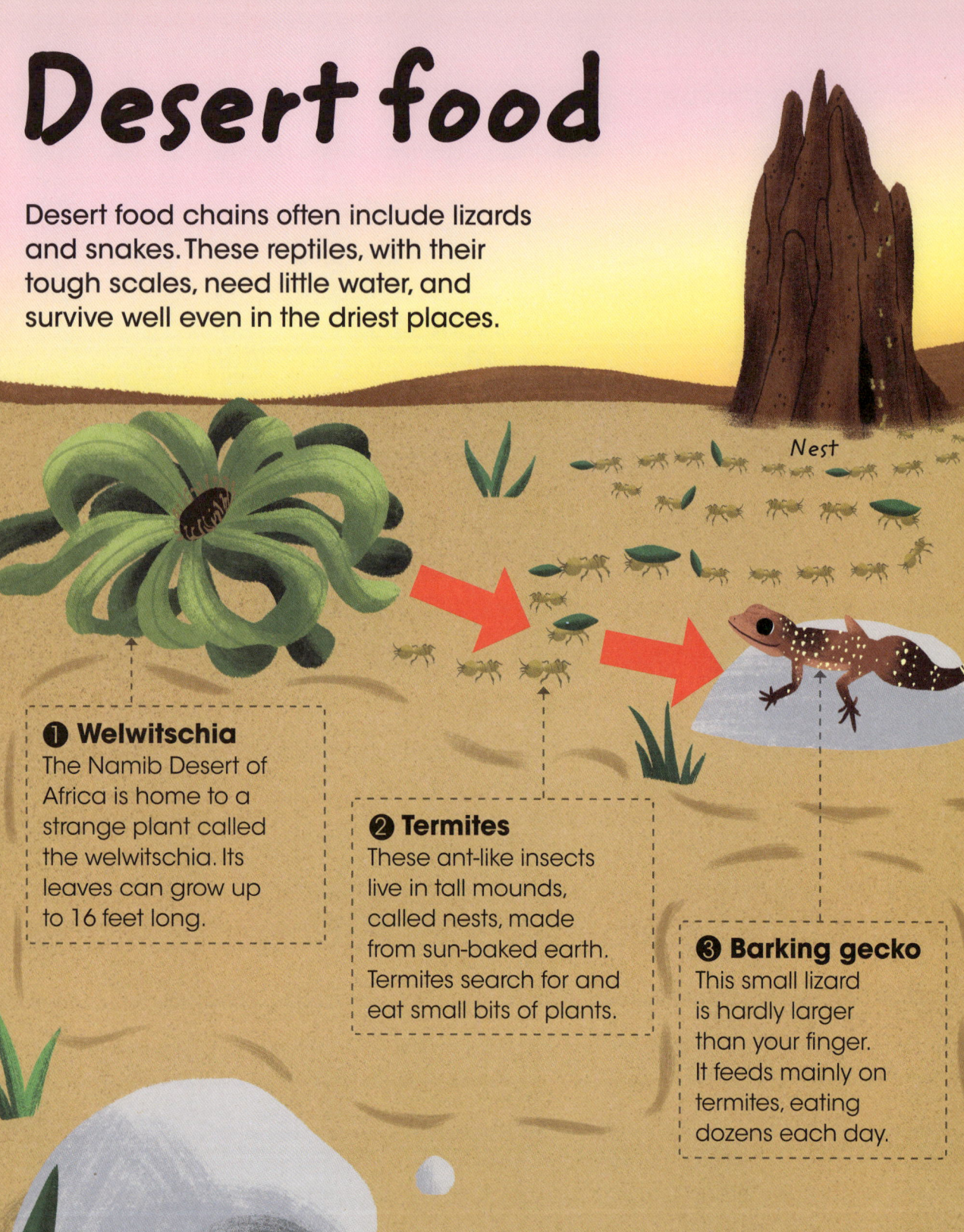

Nest

Rock

❶ Welwitschia
The Namib Desert of Africa is home to a strange plant called the welwitschia. Its leaves can grow up to 16 feet long.

❷ Termites
These ant-like insects live in tall mounds, called nests, made from sun-baked earth. Termites search for and eat small bits of plants.

❸ Barking gecko
This small lizard is hardly larger than your finger. It feeds mainly on termites, eating dozens each day.

Camel

ANIMAL FACT FILE

- **Animal group:** Mammal
- **Height:** 6.5 feet
- **Habitat:** Deserts, grasslands, scrub
- **Main foods:** Plants
- **In danger?:** Bactrian—yes, dromedary—not yet

A camel can drink 80 gallons of water in 3 minutes!

Dromedary camel

The one-humped camel, or dromedary, is found in hot and sandy deserts in Africa and the Middle East.

Long eyelashes help keep sand and dust out of the camel's eyes.

Its tough mouth can chew all kinds of desert plants, even those with thorns and spines.

Wide, padded feet stop the dromedary camel from sinking into the soft desert sand.

The dromedary camel has a short coat of fur.

Bactrian camel

Its humps are mainly fat!

The two-humped, or bactrian, camel is from cold and mostly rocky deserts in Asia.

A camel's body temperature can rise by several degrees without making it sweat, which saves water.

The bactrian camel has a thick, shaggy coat in winter that it sheds when temperatures rise.

Its nostrils can close to keep out sand and dust.

The bactrian camel has hard, tough feet that can withstand stones and rocks.

Do you know your camels? Check the boxes to match the correct type of camel to the descriptions.

	Dromedary	Bactrian
I have one hump.	☐	☐
My fur is long and shaggy.	☐	☐
My feet are wide and padded.	☐	☐
I live in cold, mostly rocky deserts.	☐	☐

Super-senses

Desert animals have amazing senses that help them find food and avoid dangers.

Hyper-hearing!

The **fennec fox** has huge ears to hear the tiny sounds of its prey, including mice, beetles, and ants.

The **desert golden mole** uses its long whiskers and thick fur to pick up movements of worms or insects nearby.

Mega motion detection!

Smells by tasting!

The **desert death adder** flicks out its tongue to collect tiny smells floating in the air. Then it tastes the smell in its mouth.

Heat sense!

The **Mongolian pit viper** has holes, called pits, between its eyes and nostrils. The pits detect heat from animals, so the snake can find its prey in darkness.

The **spotted hyena's** large nose follows the scents of antelopes, gazelles, and other creatures. It can also smell a dead animal from miles away.

Super-smell!

A hyena's sense of smell is 100 times better than mine!

Join the dots to find another desert animal with super-hearing!

Temperate woods

Temperate woodlands are always busy with life! They have warm summers, cool winters, and steady amounts of rain throughout the year.

Spring
It is warm and bright. Tree leaves grow, and flowers cover the woodland floor. Many animals become more active. They feed hungrily.

The leaves are wide and flat.

The **jay** gets ready to make a nest and raise a family.

The **red fox** mother stays in her den (burrow) with her new babies, called kits. The father brings food.

The **peacock butterfly** has woken up after her winter sleep. She lays her eggs on nettles.

Tree feasts

In a woodland, the trees provide most food. So the food chains start with buds, flowers, leaves, fruits, roots, shoots, bark—even solid wood!

The **wildcat** hunts many creatures, including mice, squirrels, birds, and even the weasel.

Wood pigeons peck apart and swallow acorns as fast as they can.

Squirrels eat some acorns and bury others to eat later.

The **great tit** feeds on acorns, including any bugs in them.

The **acorn moth grub** munches its way into an acorn.

The **sparrowhawk** preys on small woodland birds.

The **weasel** hunts mice, voles, and similar small mammals.

Deathwatch beetle grubs chew the wood, making tunnels deep into the tree.

Wood mice nibble acorns when they fall to the ground.

Wow! Just one oak tree can be home and food for more than 400 creatures!

Go wild with this wildcat mask!

① With the help of an adult, cut a cat's face from a paper plate or piece of cardboard. Color it in.

② Make holes for the whiskers. Poke drinking straws through the holes, and glue them in place on the inside.

③ Make two holes, one on each side. Tie a piece of elastic through the holes. Now wear your mask and be a cool cat!

Moose

Male moose shed their antlers in winter to save energy. A new set regrows in spring.

At breeding time, male moose make a bellowing noise!

It's so loud that it can be heard 2 miles away!

This hump stores extra energy in the form of fat.

Moose have no upper front teeth. But the tough top lip and sharp lower front teeth easily bite plant foods.

Under the moose's chin is a flap of skin and fur, called a dewlap.

ANIMAL FACT FILE

Animal group: Mammal

Height: 6.5 ft

Habitat: Woodlands, forests

Where in the world: North America, Europe, North Asia

Main foods: Leaves, twigs, buds, fruits

In danger?: Not yet

Life underground

Holes, burrows, and tunnels are made by many woodland creatures. Some burrowers are as small as earthworms, others as big as badgers.

Badgers live in a network of burrows called a sett.

Earthworms eat their way through soil, taking in tiny bits of food.

The male badger is called a boar, the female is a sow, and the youngsters are cubs.

The nest chamber is at the end of a tunnel.

Giant panda

ANIMAL FACT FILE

 Animal group: Mammal

 Length: 5 feet long

 Habitat: Bamboo woods

 Where in the world: East Asia

 Main foods: Bamboos

 In danger?: Yes—endangered

A panda's paw has five clawed fingers, plus an extra bone that works like a thumb.

The giant panda has long, sharp teeth suited to eating meat, yet it mostly eats plants!

The giant panda eats bamboo, which is a kind of grass that grows as tall as trees.

A panda spends most of its day chewing bamboo leaves and stems.

Did you know that there are probably fewer than 3,000 wild giant pandas left?

A mother panda has one cub at a time. It is tiny when born—smaller than your fist!

Color the shapes to match the colored dots to reveal a little cub.

Giant pandas sometimes eat other foods, such as fish, frogs, and eggs.

Deep sleep

Winter in woodlands is cold and rainy. One way to survive is just to sleep right through it! This is called hibernation.

In New Zealand, when it is very cold, the **short-tailed bat** sleeps in a tree hole or cave.

In Europe, the **hedgehog** makes a nest under a woodland bush or log.

In Australia, the **striped burrowing frog** digs down into the woodland soil and stays there.

ZZZZZzzz

Sometimes a hibernating hedgehog is joined by some friends!

Rivers and lakes

Freshwater habitats can vary from speedy streams to wide rivers, from little ponds to vast lakes, and from cold marshes to tropical swamps!

Look! The river starts as a few shallow streams, flowing into one.

Yes, and as more streams join, the river gets wider!

The **water vole** lives in a burrow in the river bank. It eats leaves, grass, waterweeds, and other plants.

The **kingfisher** sits on a branch above the river, watching for fish. Then it dives like an arrow into the water to catch its meal.

The **dipper** walks along the stream bed, as it pecks among the pebbles for worms and bugs.

Join the dots to see which big white bird lives on the lake.

The **perch** hunts small fish, tadpoles, and other water creatures. It even crunches up freshwater shellfish.

The **grayling** noses in the stream bed for water insects and worms. It also eats bits of leaves and plants.

The **pochard** dips its head under the water or even swims down to reach waterweeds and small creatures.

Super-swimmers

Moving in water uses more energy and muscle power than moving on land. So most creatures have streamlined bodies that slip easily through the water, and fins, flippers, or webbed feet to push themselves along.

The **otter** has flaps of skin between its toes (webs). It chases fish, frogs, and other prey.

Tail for steering

Long, slender body

Long, smooth, scaly body

Side fins for steering

The African goliath frog is the world's largest frog!

The **trout** curves its body and tail from side to side to push against the water, using its fins to change direction.

The **black-throated diver** kicks its webbed feet and flaps its wings as it swims after fish and frogs.

Long, sharp beak

Small paddle-like wings

Large webbed feet

I'll take a photograph!

Powerful back legs

Webs

The **African goliath frog** swims by kicking its huge, strong back feet, with long toes joined by webs.

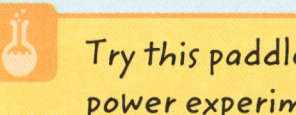

Try this paddle power experiment!

Part-fill a bowl, basin, or sink with water. Move your hand through the water, fingers spread. Feel how much water you can push.

Put your hand in a small plastic bag and do the same.

Feel how much more water you push. That's why webbed feet are good for swimming fast.

Hippopotamus

ANIMAL FACT FILE

 Animal group: Mammal

 Length: 13 feet

 Habitat: Rivers and lakes

 Where in the world: Central and southern Africa

 Main foods: Grass and water plants

 In danger?: Yes—vulnerable

Most mammals have fur or hair. But the hippo has almost none, apart from whiskers on the snout.

The hippo has huge, tusk-like canine teeth. It uses them for fighting to be boss of the herd, and for defense against predators.

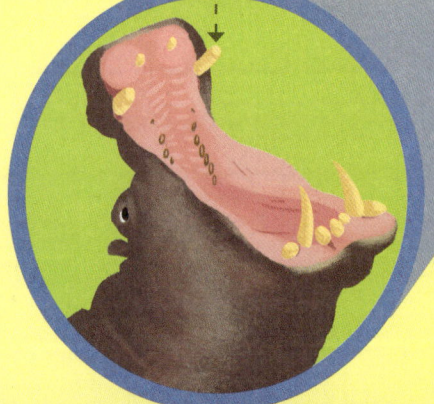

The hippo uses its wide, bendy lips to pull up plants such as grasses, which it then chews with its cheek teeth.

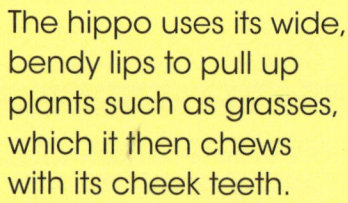

Little and large

Some freshwater fish are as long as a car, others are smaller than your fingertip. Take a look at a few of the most interesting!

Piranha
Size: 10 inches long
Piranhas live in shoals (groups) and have a fierce bite, so they can attack animals much larger than themselves.

Common eel
Size: 3 feet long
The common eel has two small front fins, and one long fin that goes along its back and around its tail to the underside.

Large, blade-like, razor-sharp teeth

The eel's snake-like body has very tiny scales

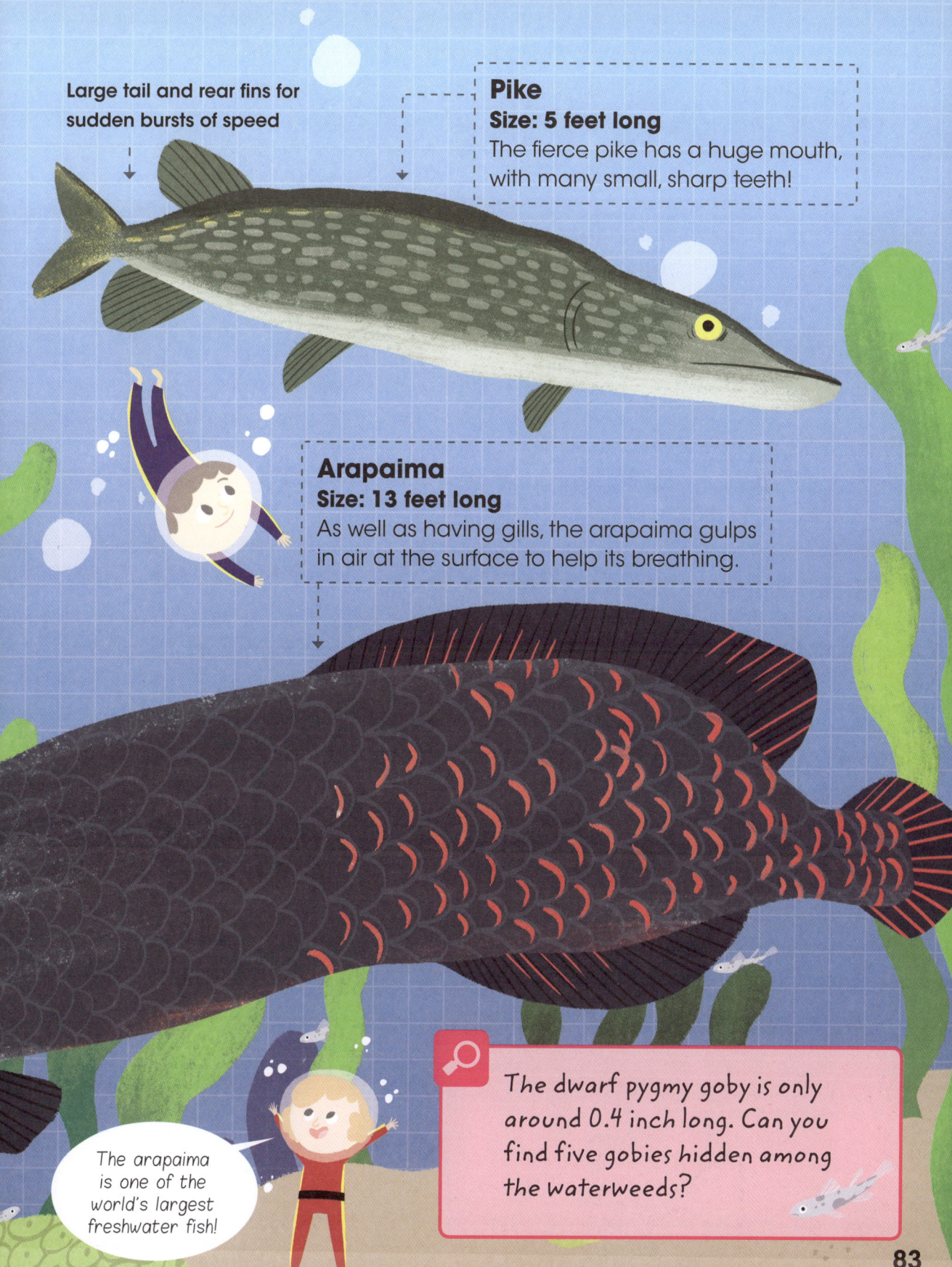

Nile crocodile

ANIMAL FACT FILE

- **Animal group:** Reptile
- **Length:** 5 feet
- **Habitat:** Rivers, lakes, swamps
- **Where in the world:** Africa
- **Main foods:** All kinds of animals, from fish to zebras
- **In danger?:** Not yet

The crocodile has thick skin and scales. Only lions, leopards, and hyenas can bite through these.

The crocodile's eyes, ears, and nostrils are on the top of its head, so it can float low in the water, yet still see, hear, and breathe.

It has 60 to 70 pointed teeth in its long jaws!

Changing shape

Some creatures live in water when young. Then, as they grow up, they change shape, and start living on land or up in the air!

A dragonfly lays over 1,500 eggs!

Dragonfly life cycle

❶ Eggs
A dragonfly begins life as a tiny egg—on, in, or under the leaf of a water plant.

❷ Young nymph
The egg hatches into a nymph. It has gills, six legs, and a big, strong mouth.

❸ Nymph
The nymph sheds its skin and grows a new, bigger one. It does this several times over two or three years, then crawls up a reed stem into the air.

❹ Adult dragonfly
The skin splits for the last time, and out comes the four-winged adult dragonfly. It is a swift hunter of flies, gnats, and similar creatures.

❶ **Frogspawn**
A frog begins life as a jelly-covered egg in a big lump of eggs called frogspawn.

❷ **Young tadpole**
The egg hatches into a tadpole. It has gills, a big head, and a wriggly tail.

Frog life cycle

❹ **Adult frog**
It is now a grown-up frog that can live in water or on land. It feeds on all kinds of worms, bugs, and insects.

❸ **Tadpole**
The tadpole grows back legs, then front legs. Its gills and tail shrink. It develops lungs to breathe air.

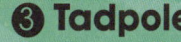

The change in body shape is known as metamorphosis.

Color the frog to complete the transformation!

Conifer trees

Conifer forests have a short, warm summer and a long, snowy winter. Some of the world's fiercest animals live here.

Conifer forest trees include pines, firs, and spruces.

Summer

In summer, the **elk** munches on buds and shoots.

The **sable** hunts mice, rats, voles, lemmings, and other small prey.

The **capercaillie** feeds on the ground, eating bugs, worms, and shoots.

The **taiga vole** chomps on most kinds of plant foods in summer.

Help these animals find their way through the trees to their favorite winter foods.

Winter

In winter, the **elk** searches for mosses and ferns to eat. It scrapes away snow with its hooves.

The **sable** comes out of its winter burrow now and then to hunt small animals.

The **capercaillie** feeds in the trees, pecking conifer leaves, buds, and seeds.

The **taiga vole** eats grass, horsetails, and other plants.

Beaver lodge

Beavers build a winter home, called a lodge. Even when ice covers their pool, they can swim out, gather their stored food, and take it back to eat!

Beavers make a pool by building a dam across the stream.

The lodge is very strong and has an underwater entrance to keep out predators, such as wolves and lynx.

The dam and lodge are made of sticks, twigs, stones, and mud!

The beaver family have stored food, such as twigs, bark, and stems, in their watery pool.

Build a beaver lodge!

1

Gather your supplies: long, thin items like drinking straws, lollipop sticks, and cocktail sticks, plus tissue paper.

First, bend some straws into a C-shaped framework. Then weave the other items in and out. Use wet tissue paper to hold everything in place. Put this on a sheet of blue paper.

Shape some beavers from brown modeling clay. Don't forget the wide, flat tail!

Siberian tiger

ANIMAL FACT FILE

 Animal group: Mammal

 Length: 10 feet, including tail

 Habitat: Conifer forests, mountains

 Where in the world: East Asia

 Main foods: Deer, boar, rabbits, other mammals

 In danger?: Yes—endangered

The Siberian tiger is the world's largest big cat. Males weigh over 440 pounds, and females up to 330 pounds.

Tigers use their long front teeth, called canines, to kill their prey.

The tiger's whiskers help it feel its way at night, when it hunts.

Pack on the prowl

Conifer forests are home to one of the world's most widespread and feared predators—the gray wolf. Most gray wolves live in family groups called packs.

❶ Members of the pack hunt together. The main hunters are the chief adults, called the alpha male and alpha female.

❷ The wolves prey on the old, young, injured, or sick. They surround the victim, then dash in, biting it around the rear end.

❸ The alpha pair eats first. The others wait their turn, before feeding on what is left: often just skin, gristle, and bones.

Grizzly bear

The grizzly bear is a large kind of brown bear. It has pale tips to its hairs, making it look old or "grizzled."

It often stands on its back legs to get a better view, smell the air, and find food or detect danger.

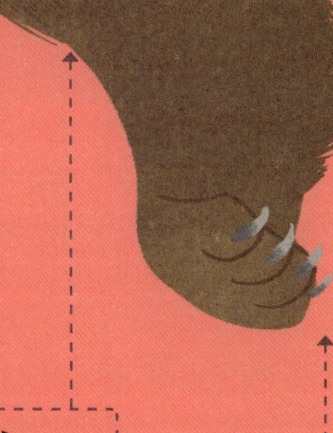

ANIMAL FACT FILE

Animal group: Mammal
Height: 10 feet, standing
Habitat: Forests, woods, mountains
Where in the world: North America
Main foods: Almost anything
In danger?: Not yet

Grizzly bears feed hungrily in autumn. They store the extra energy as body fat.

The long, curved claws can swipe and scoop salmon and other fish from the water.

The grizzly bear eats almost anything—from roots, shoots, fruits, leaves, and berries, to fish, rabbits, hares, wild pigs, goats, sheep, deer, and bee honey.

In autumn, a grizzly bear can eat more than 30 salmon in one day!

How many salmon fish are jumbled up in this grizzly's great feast?

Fly in, fly out

Summer visits can be very short.

Winter is so long and cold in conifer forests that many birds leave. Each year, they arrive in spring, feed and raise their young in summer, and leave in autumn!

Spring

The **Siberian thrush** flies in from warmer southern areas.

The **bean goose** usually lands in the same area each year. It looks for its old nesting site near water.

The **yellow warbler** reaches the conifer forest in April or May.

Summer

The Siberian thrush makes its nest in a bush or small tree.

The bean goose nest is a small scrape or hollow under a shrub or bush.

Grab a piece of paper and make your own flying bird!

Launch your bird and see how far it flies!

1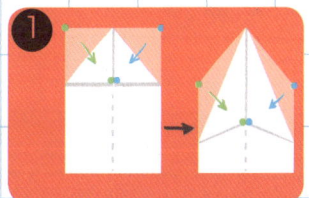
Fold top corners into the center line. Then fold in again.

2
Fold in half lengthways. Fold down to make wings.

3
Draw on the bird's beak, eyes, and feathers.

Autumn

The Siberian thrush leaves in September. It flies more than 1,200 miles to South Asia.

As the days become shorter and colder, bean geese prepare for their migration 1,800 miles south.

By July, the yellow warblers are ready to leave. They may fly more than 900 miles.

Some yellow warblers stay less than three months!

The yellow warbler makes a small cup-shaped nest in a tree.

Seas and oceans

Seas and oceans are saltwater habitats. They vary from small, shallow, sheltered bays to vast, deep, stormy oceans.

Limpets cling tightly to the rocks as they feed on tiny plants.

The continental shelf is the area of seabed around most land, about 300–650 feet deep.

The seashore is a harsh habitat—bashed by big waves, heated by the sun, soaked with rain, and covered by high tides.

The **lobster** lurks in a cave and grabs passing victims.

Can you find these sea creatures? Write their names below.

Starfish use their "arms" to pull apart shellfish before eating them.

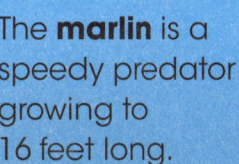

surface water

The ocean surface waters are light, illuminated by sunlight.

The **marlin** is a speedy predator growing to 16 feet long.

The **Portuguese man o' war** is a group of jellyfish-like animals with a "sail."

The ocean's mid water becomes darker and colder.

mid water

The **megamouth shark** opens its jaws wide to swallow any kind of food.

Cod form large shoals (groups) that prey on any smaller creatures.

The **deep-sea angler** has a light on its head to attract victims.

On the deep seabed, it is totally black and almost ice-cold.

deep seabed

101

Across the ocean

Some sea creatures travel farther than any land animal. Many have no nests, dens, or regular homes. They roam for thousands of miles across the open ocean.

The **bottlenose dolphin** swims south in winter to warmer waters, then north again for the summer. Some of these journeys are more than 1,000 miles.

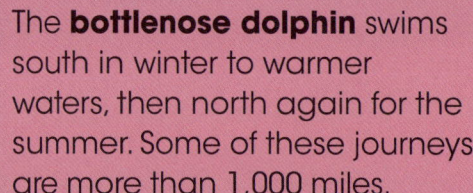

How do sea animals find their way across vast oceans?

Pacific Ocean

North America

Atlantic Ocean

The **gray whale** spends summer in cold but food-rich northern Pacific waters, and winter in warmer waters near the tropics. It's a yearly journey of over 12,000 miles.

South America

Atlantic Ocean

The female **blue shark** travels across the Atlantic, from America to Europe, to have her babies. She then travels south to Africa, and back across the Atlantic to where she started—a round trip of 9,000 miles.

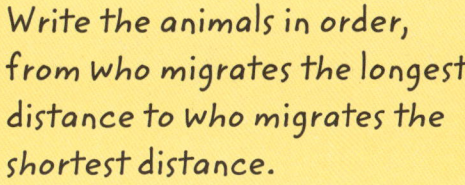

Write the animals in order, from who migrates the longest distance to who migrates the shortest distance.

1. gray whale
2. ....
3. ....
4. ....
5. dugong

They use positions of the Sun, Moon, and stars to help them find their way!

The **dugong** or sea cow is about 10 feet long. It swims over 600 miles each year to feed on seagrass and other plants, always staying near the coast.

Europe

Africa

Asia

Indian Ocean

Australia

Pacific Ocean

The **green turtle** slowly wanders the ocean, flapping its flippers, to search for jellyfish and plants. In one year it can cover more than 3,500 miles.

103

Great white shark

Water out through gill slits

Water flows over gills

Water in through mouth

Great white sharks can swim fast, but they cannot turn quickly or slow down suddenly.

The great white can detect the tiniest drops of blood in water. It follows the trail to a sick or injured victim.

ANIMAL FACT FILE

 Animal group: Fish

 Length: 20 feet

 Habitat: Coast to open sea

 Where in the world: All but the coldest oceans

 Main foods: Fish, seabirds, seals, dolphins, whales—anything!

 In danger?: Yes—vulnerable

It's a good thing they can't turn quickly!

Between the tides

The seashore is an in-between habitat. It's dry when the tide is out and wet when the tide comes in. This happens twice each day, every day.

Low tide

The rocky shore animals hide away or close up. They must cope with sun, wind, rain, or even snow.

Mussels cling to the rock using strong, stretchy threads.

Beadlet anemones close up their tentacles when the tide is out.

Beadlet anemones look like jelly blobs at low tide!

Blue whale

Blue whales "sing" by making clicks, squeaks, and wails!

ANIMAL FACT FILE

 Animal group: Mammal

 Length: 100 feet

 Habitat: Open sea

 Where in the world: All oceans, even polar regions

 Main foods: Krill and other small creatures

 In danger?: Yes—endangered

On top of the whale's head are its blowholes (its breathing nostrils). They blow out old, stale air and take in fresh air.

Whale flippers are like our arms—they have bones inside. They can turn to steer when swimming.

Whale flukes are not like our legs—they do not have bones inside. They are mainly muscle.

The blue whale's throat has skin grooves or creases, called pleats.

Carefully cut out small krill shapes from cardboard and put them in a sink full of water. Try using a kitchen sieve like a whale's baleen to scoop up the food. Can you catch them all in one try?

Whale calls travel miles through the sea!

Long, brush-like parts, called baleen, hang from the whale's upper jaw, to sieve food from the water.

Blue whales eat small shrimp-like creatures called krill.

Battle of the giants

Many of the world's largest predators live in the ocean. When they meet, each must decide whether to attack and make a feast of its enemy, or leave to find smaller prey.

KILLER WHALE

HEADS Length: 30 feet
TAILS Senses: 8/10

The killer whale is actually the biggest kind of dolphin. Its teeth lock together so no victim can escape.

Round 1

Winner: ....

TIGER SHARK

HEADS Length: 15 feet
TAILS Senses: 9/10

The tiger shark is one of the largest and fiercest sharks. It attacks and eats almost any prey!

GIANT SPIDER CRAB

HEADS Pincers: 10
TAILS Width: 10 feet

The giant spider crab has spindly pincers. It feeds on dead and dying creatures.

Round 2

Winner: ....

LION'S MANE JELLYFISH

HEADS Tentacles: 100 +
TAILS Width: 6 feet

The lion's mane jellyfish is the biggest jellyfish, with stinging tentacles over 65 feet long.

SPERM WHALE

HEADS Length: 65 feet
TAILS Eye size: 3 inches

The sperm whale is the world's largest predator. It has big cone-shaped teeth in its lower jaw.

Round 3

Winner:

....

COLOSSAL SQUID

HEADS Length: 40 feet
TAILS Eye size: 10 inches

The colossal squid is the world's largest invertebrate. Its tentacles have suckers with sharp hooks.

Play "Battle of the giants" with a friend! You'll need a coin and a pencil.

❶ Pick your team: red or blue.

❷ For each round, flip a coin to see what feature will win the battle.

❸ Write the winner's name in the box.

❹ Whoever wins the most rounds is the champion!

Champion:

....

Write the champion's name on the trophy and color it in!

Tundra

Winter

Tundra is land that is frozen for much of the year. It is too cold for trees to grow, but low plants grow in the short summer.

The **rock ptarmigan** pecks up any bits of plant food, including seeds, stems, and roots.

The **stoat** searches for small creatures such as mice, voles, and lemmings.

The **snowshoe hare** eats twigs, bark from trees, and buds from plants and flowers.

In the winter, white fur and feathers blend into the snow and ice!

Summer

Tundra swans feed on the plants, make nests, and raise their chicks. In just a few weeks, they will fly south on their winter migration.

Melted ice and snow forms pools of water where **mosquitoes** and other insects breed by the billions.

But, look! In the summer, they shed their white coats and grow brown ones instead!

Can you spot a...

rock ptarmigan?

stoat?

snowshoe hare?

Big and small

The tundra is a dangerous place for plant-eaters, because predators are always hungry. These two animals, one big and one small, have different ways to avoid becoming prey.

Among the biggest tundra animals are musk oxen. Some weigh over 600 pounds!

Musk oxen live in small groups, called herds, usually from five to ten, but sometimes up to fifty.

Musk oxen

When in danger, adults stand in a circle around their young, known as calves, to protect them.

Both male and females have horns. They use them to scare enemies, and to battle each other to be boss of the herd.

One of the smallest tundra mammals is the tundra vole. It is only 6 inches long.

The tundra vole is a rodent—cousin of mice, rats, hamsters, and gerbils.

When in danger, tundra voles race to their nest burrow. They may block the entrance with earth to keep out predators.

Its long, sharp front teeth never stop growing!

Tundra vole

These three voles want to get back to their own nest burrows. Can you help them find the right tunnels?

Snowy owl

Its eyes see well in the dark. The owl moves its head from side to side to figure out how far away things are.

The owl's hearing is amazing—it can even hear hidden prey burrowing under the snow.

An adult male has white plumage (feathers), while the female and youngsters have brown markings.

ANIMAL FACT FILE

Animal group: Bird
Height: 20 inches
Habitat: Tundra, rocky areas, coasts, and grasslands
Where in the world: North America, Europe, and Asia
Main foods: Small creatures such as lemmings, voles, mice, birds
In danger?: Not yet

Happy families

The tundra summer is so short that animals raise their families fast. Youngsters must grow up quickly to survive the long, cold winter ahead!

The Arctic tern flies from the Arctic to the Antarctic and back each year.

Pikas may look like mice, but they are cousins of rabbits and hares. A female and male have four or five babies in late spring.

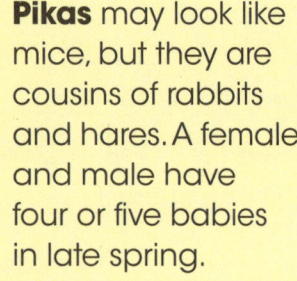

An **Arctic tern** lays two eggs in a nest lined with grass and moss, near the coast. Both parents attack any creature that comes near the eggs or chicks.

Draw your own family photo!

The **Arctic hare** does not have a nest burrow. Instead, it shelters among plants. The female has up to 10 babies, called leverets.

The **snow bunting's** eggs hatch in less than two weeks, and the chicks can fly only two weeks later!

Caribou

ANIMAL FACT FILE

- **Animal group:** Mammal
- **Height:** 5 feet
- **Habitat:** Tundra, conifer forests
- **Where in the world:** North America, Europe, and Asia
- 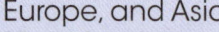 **Main foods:** Leaves, grasses, lichens, moss, and other plants
- **In danger?:** Not yet

Both male and female caribou have antlers. In all other deer, the female lacks antlers.

Each year, the caribou grows new antlers. They develop in the spring or summer, and fall off in autumn or winter.

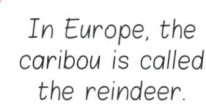

In Europe, the caribou is called the reindeer.

The long hairs of the caribou's outer coat are hollow to help keep the cold out and body warmth in.

Caribou click as they walk! The sound is made by bones and joints in their feet. It may help the herd stay together when it is dark.

Put your hands over your eyes. Ask a friend to walk around the room, snapping their fingers every five seconds. Point to where you think they are. Were you right?

In summer, the hooves are wide and soft for walking in the swampy tundra ground.

In winter, the hooves become hard and sharp-edged to grip snow and ice.

Mountain tundra

As you go up a mountain, it gets colder and windier. Up high, there is alpine (mountain) tundra. It is home to some of the world's best climbers.

Above the mountain tundra, it is too cold and windy for plants. There are just bare rocks and the snowy mountain top.

Soaring in the sky is the **bearded vulture**. Its main food is carrion—the bodies of animals that have died.

For every 3,000 feet you go straight up, the temperature drops by 50°F!

No wonder alpine tundra is rarely warmer than 50°F, even in summer.

At breeding time, male **black grouse** strut, show off their feathers, and make loud calls to attract females.

Alpine marmots can dig their burrow in soil that is very hard or even frozen.

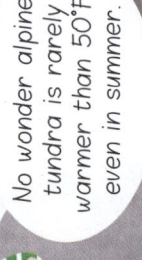

Chamois are goat-antelopes. They have strong legs and hooves to leap through alpine grass and over rocks.

Below the mountain tundra, conifer trees grow. They are covered with thick snow in winter.

Apollo butterflies feed on nectar from flowers, which only bloom for a few days in mid summer.

True or false? Check the boxes.

TRUE FALSE

Apollo butterflies feed on flower nectar.

The bearded vulture eats mainly dead bodies.

Female black grouse show off to attract males.

Glossary

Amphibians Cold-blooded animals without scaly skin that can live in water or on land.

Birds Warm-blooded animals with feathers, wings, and a beak. They lay eggs that hatch into chicks. Many make nests for their eggs.

Breed To make more of an animal's kind. Some animals lay eggs. Others give birth to babies.

Camouflage A color, pattern, or shape of an animal that helps it blend in with its surroundings.

Canopy The uppermost branches of the trees in a forest.

Carnivore A class of animals that feeds on the flesh of other animals.

Cold-blooded Cold-blooded animals become hotter when it is hot outside and cooler when it is cold outside.

Down The soft, fine, fluffy feathers or hair that form the insulating undercoat layer.

Emergent The tallest trees in a forest, which grow above the canopy.

Feathers Soft structures growing from a bird's skin and forming its plumage.

Filter-feed Feeding by filtering or sieving out tiny plankton or nutrients floating in the water.

Fish Animals with scaly skin, gills for breathing underwater, and fins and a tail for swimming. They live in water.

Food chain A series of individual plants or animals, each dependent on the next as a source of food.

Freshwater Relating to or living in freshwater—the water in rivers and lakes.

Habitat A type of place where an animal or plant lives. It provides the right conditions for that living thing to thrive, such as food, temperature, and amount of water.

Herbivore A class of animals that doesn't feed on flesh, but that eats only vegetable or plant matter.

Hibernation A deep sleep that some animals enter to conserve energy and survive harsh conditions.

Insulation Not allowing heat or cold to pass through.

Invertebrate An animal without a backbone. Worms, insects, spiders, crabs, and starfish are invertebrates.

Mammals Warm-blooded animals with fur or hair that produce milk to feed their babies. Humans are mammals—so are dogs and dolphins.

Metamorphosis Changing shape greatly when growing from young to adult—for example, a caterpillar changing into a butterfly.

Migration A seasonal movement of animals from one place to another.

Omnivore A type of animal that gets energy from eating both the flesh of other animals and plants or vegetables. Humans are omnivores.

Pinniped A carnivorous aquatic mammal, such as a seal or walrus.

Plumage The layer of feathers covering the body of a bird.

Predator A meat-eating animal that hunts and kills other animals to eat. The animals it hunts are known as prey.

Prey An animal that is hunted and killed for food by another animal. The animal that hunts it is known as a predator.

Primate A mammal distinguished by having hand-like feet and forward-facing eyes. Monkeys, apes, and humans are primates.

Reptiles Cold-blooded animals that have dry, scaly skin, and that lay eggs on land. Snakes, lizards, crocodiles, and turtles are all types of reptile.

Saltwater Relating to or living in saltwater—the water in the sea.

Scales Tough, overlapping plates that cover and protect the skin of reptiles and fish.

Senses An animal's senses tell it about the world around it.

Shoal A large number of fish swimming together.

Undercoat An inner layer of short, fine fur or down underlying an animal's outer fur or feathers, providing warmth and waterproofing.

Understory The lower branches of the trees in a forest.

Venom A harmful liquid made by some predators to help them kill or hurt their prey. Usually injected through teeth, fangs, or a sting.

Vertebrate An animal with a backbone. Amphibians, birds, mammals, and reptiles are vertebrates.

Warm-blooded Warm-blooded animals stay the same temperature, regardless of whether it is hot or cold outside.

Index

A
acorn moth grub 66
African elephant 30-1
African goliath frog 78, 79
African wild dog 29
alpine marmot 122
Amazon horned frog 19
amphibians 8-9
animal kingdom 8-9
Antarctic 41
apes 20-1, 22-3
Apollo butterfly 123
Arabian oryx 54
arapaima 83
Arctic 40-1, 42, 46
Arctic fox 43
Arctic hare 119
Arctic tern 118
autumn 65, 99

B
badger 70-1
bank vole 65, 71
barbet 17
barking gecko 58
barnacle 107
bat 74-5
beadlet anemone 106, 107
bean goose 98-9
bearded vulture 122
bears 44-5, 75, 96-7
beaver lodges 90-1
beluga whale 42-3
bird-dropping caterpillar 18
black-backed jackal 59
black bear 75
black grouse 122
black-throated diver 79
blue shark 103
blue whale 108-9

boa constrictor 12
bottlenose dolphin 102
breeding 6, 68, 95, 118-19
budgerigar 54
burrows 70-1
bush 27
bushbaby 14

C
camels 60-1
camouflage 18-19, 39, 45, 105
capercaillie 88-9
caribou 120-1
cassowary 57
centipede 14
chameleon 19
chamois 123
cheetah 34-5
chinstrap penguin 41
cod 101
colossal squid 111
common eel 82
conifer forests 11, 88-99
continental shelf 100
cubs 45, 95

D
dams 90-1
darkling beetle 37, 53
deathwatch beetle grub 67
deep-sea angler 101
desert death adder 62
desert golden mole 62
deserts 10, 52-63
dipper 76
dormouse 75
dragonfly 86
dry season 26
dugong 103
dwarf pygmy goby 83

E
eagle owl 53
earthworm 8, 70
eating 6
eggs 56, 86, 87
elk 68-9, 88-9
emperor penguin 48-9
emu 57
Equator 11

F
fangs 24
fat-tail scorpion 53
fennec fox 62
fish 8-9
flower mantis 19
flying frog 14
food chains 36-7
frogs 13-15, 19, 74, 78-9, 87
frogspawn 87
fur seal 46-7

G
gerbil 55
giant anteater 36
giant panda 72-3
giant spider crab 110
giraffe 29
Grant's gazelle 36
grass 36-7
grasslands 11, 26-39
grayling 77
grazers 28-9
great tit 66
great white shark 104-5
green turtle 103
gray kangaroo 33
gray whale 102
grizzly bear 96-7
growth 7
gyrfalcon 42

H
habitats 10-11
harp seal 46-7
harpy eagle 14
hedgehog 74
hibernation 74-5
hippopotamus 80-1
honeyguide 17
hooded seal 40
howler monkey 13

I
insects 8
insulation 43
invertebrates 8

J
jaguar 12, 36
jay 64
jerboa 53

K
killer whale 51, 110
king cobra 24-5
king penguin 51
kingfisher 76
krill 50-1, 109

L
lakes 11, 76-87
leopard 28
leopard seal 51
leverets 119
limpet 100
lion 36
lion's mane jellyfish 110
lobster 100

M
mammals 8-9
maned wolf 33
marlin 101
meat-eaters 6, 36

megamouth shark 101
metamorphosis 86–7
migration 98–9
Mongolian pit viper 63
monkeys 13, 14, 22–3
moose (elk) 68–9, 88–9
mosquito 113
mountain tundra 122–3
movement 6, 14, 28–9, 32–5, 62
musk oxen 114
mussel 106

N
Namib sidewinder 59
Nile crocodile 84–5
North Pole 41
Northern fulmar 40
Northern fur seal 46–7
nymphs 86

O
oceans 11, 100–11
orangutan 20–1
ostrich 33, 56–7
otter 78

P
pampas 26
peacock butterfly 64
peacock worm 107
perch 77
pika 118
pike 83
pinniped 46
piranha 82
plankton 50
plant-eaters 6, 36–7
pochard 77
poison dart frog 13
polar bear 44–5
polar regions 11, 40–51
Portuguese man o' war 101

prairies 26
predators 28–9
primates 22–3
pronghorn 33

R
racerunner lizard 37
red fox 64
reptiles 8–9
rhea 57
right whale 40
rivers 11, 76–87
rock ptarmigan 112–13
rodents 115

S
sable 88–9
Saharan silver ant 52
sandfish 52
savannah 27
scales 25
scarlet macaw 13
seabed 101
seals 40–1, 46–7, 51
seas 11, 50–1, 100–11
seashore 100, 106–7
secretary bird 52
senses 7, 62–3
short-tailed bat 74
Siberian thrush 98–9
Siberian tiger 92–3
silverfish 50–1
slow-worm 65
smell, sense of 62–3
snakes 12, 24–5, 59, 62–3
snow bunting 119
snowshoe hare 112–13
snowy owl 116–17
South polar skua 41
South Pole 41
Southern elephant seal 41
spadefoot toad 54
sparrowhawk 66

sperm whale 111
spider monkey 14
spotted hyena 63
spring 64, 98
squirrel 66
starfish 100
steppe eagle 36
steppe polecat 36
steppes 27
stick insect 18
stoat 112–13
striped burrowing frog 74
summer 88, 98–9, 113, 118–19
swimming 46–7

T
tadpoles 87
taiga vole 88–9
talons 117
tawny frogmouth 19
tawny owl 65
temperate woodlands 10, 64–75
termite 36–7, 58
Thomson's gazelle 29
tiger shark 110
toucan 16–17
trees 10, 11, 12–25, 66–7, 88–99
tropical rain forests 10, 12–25
trout 78
tundra 11, 112–23
tundra swan 113
tundra vole 115
tusks 31, 47

U
underground creatures 70–1

V
vertebrates 8
viscacha 55
vole 71, 76, 88–9, 115

W
walrus 46–7
warm, keeping 42–3
water sources 54–5
water vole 76
weasel 67
welwitschia 58
wet season 26
whales 40, 42–3, 51, 102, 108–11
white rhino 32
wild boar 65
wildcat 66
wildebeest 28
winter 89, 90–1, 112
wolves 33, 94–5
wood mouse 67
wood pigeon 66
woodpecker 17

Y
yellow warbler 98–9

Z
zebra 29, 38–9

Answers

Page 9
Bird, Fish, Mammal

Pages 12-13

Page 17
1—Barbet
2—Woodpecker
3—Honeyguide

Page 23
1—Monkey (howler monkey)
2—Ape (orangutan)
3—Ape (gorilla)
4—Monkey (spider monkey)

Page 27
American bison, Hyena, Saker falcon

Pages 28-29
Wildebeest—Fresh grass
African wild dogs—Home den
Thomson's gazelles—Waterhole

Page 37
Giant anteater—Termites
Darkling beetle—Grass seeds
Lion—Grant's gazelle

Page 46
False, False, True, False

Page 49
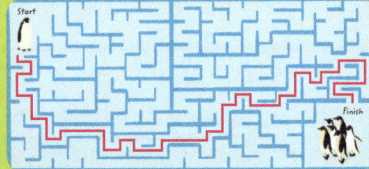

Page 51
There are 14 krill

Page 52

Page 57
Rhea—4.5 feet
Cassowary—5.5 feet
Emu—6 feet

Pages 58-59
Termites—Nest
Barking gecko—Rock
Namib sidewinder—Burrow

Page 61
Dromedary, Bactrian, Dromedary, Bactrian

Page 65

Pages 70-71

Page 73

Page 75
False, True, False

Pages 82-83

Pages 88-89

Page 97
There are 16 salmon

Page 100
Deep-sea angler, Portuguese man o' war, Limpets, Lobster

Page 103
1—Gray whale
2—Blue shark
3—Green turtle
4—Bottlenose dolphin
5—Dugong

Page 113

Page 115

Page 123
True, True, False